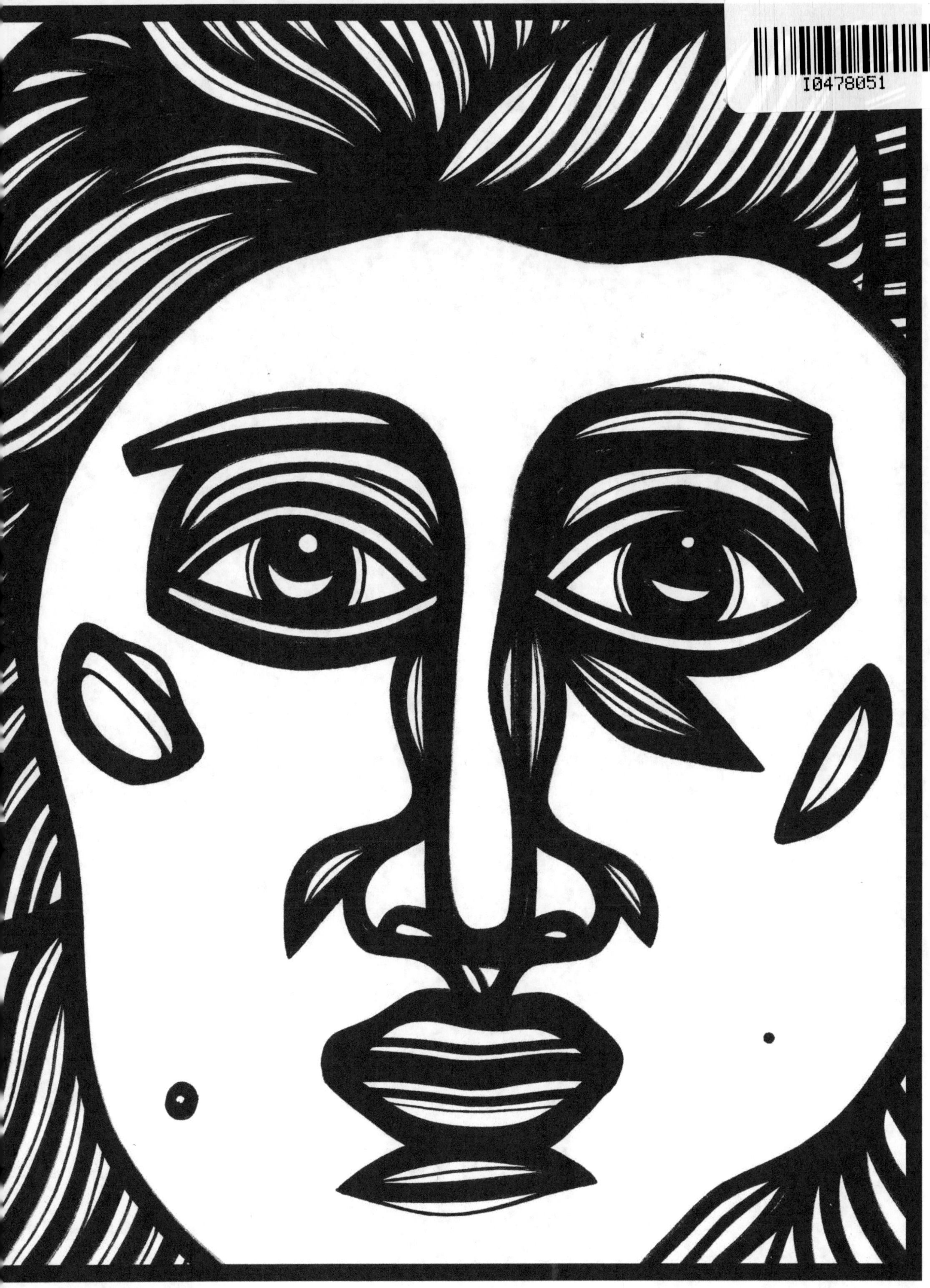

I0478051

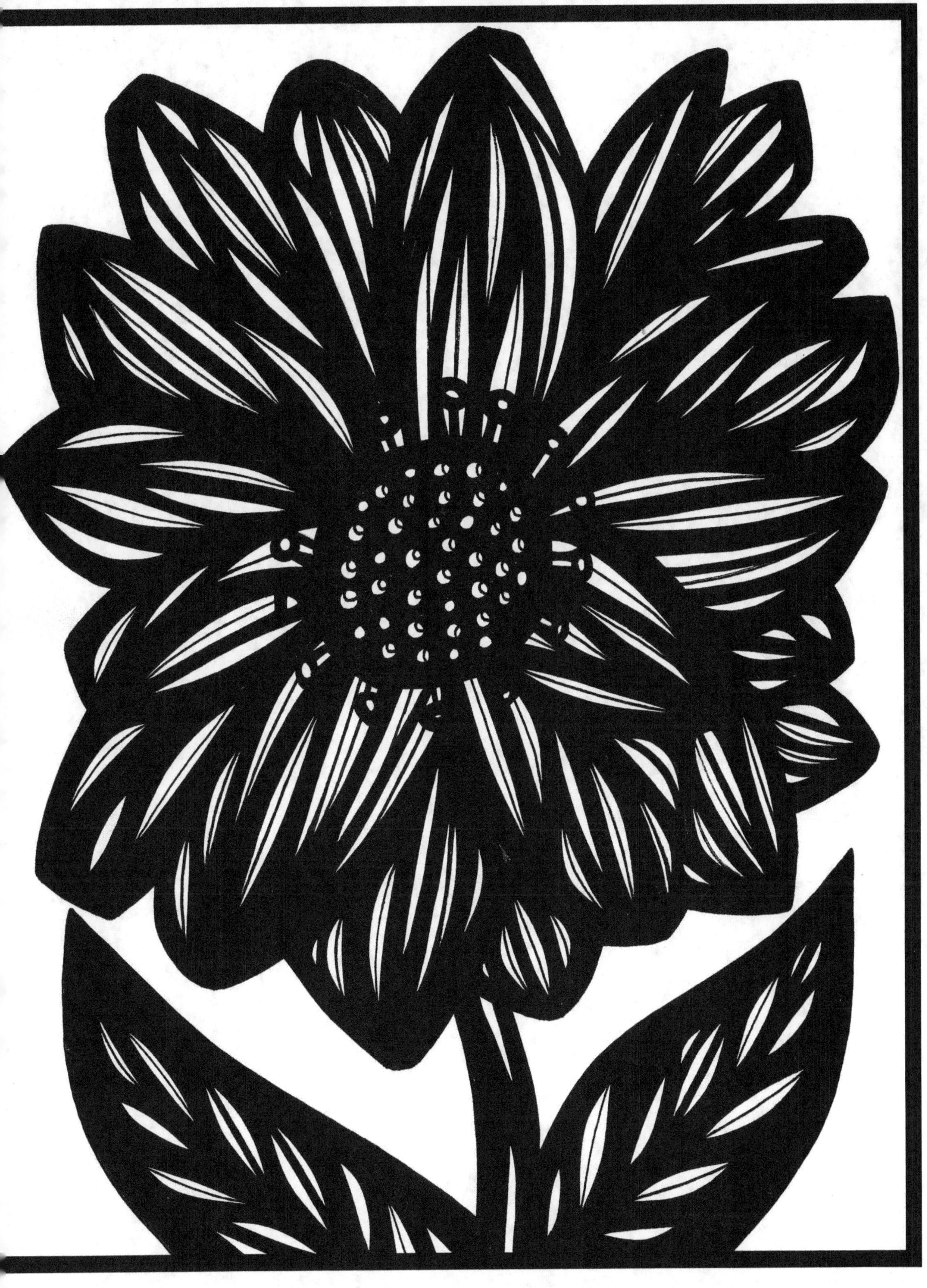

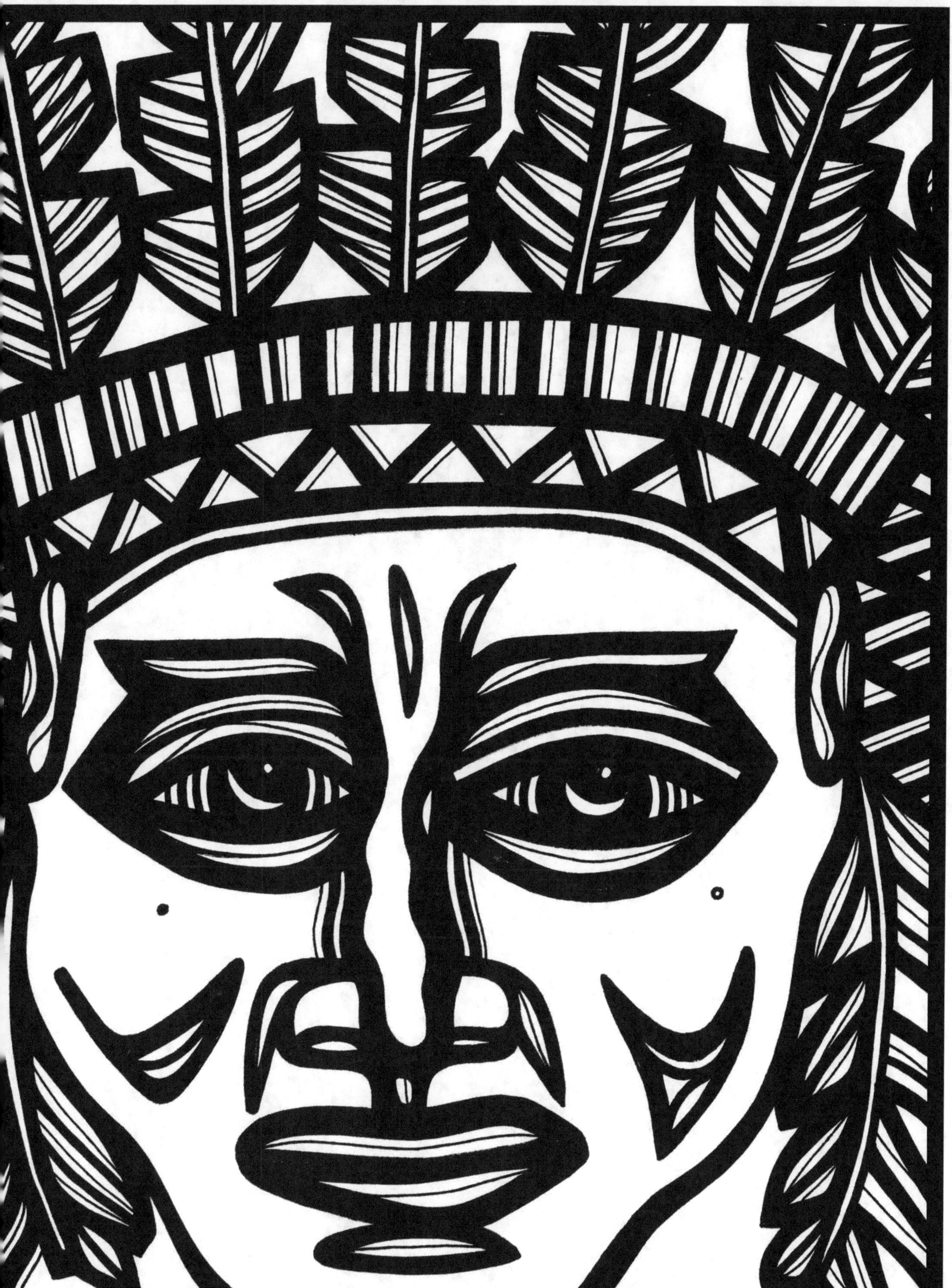

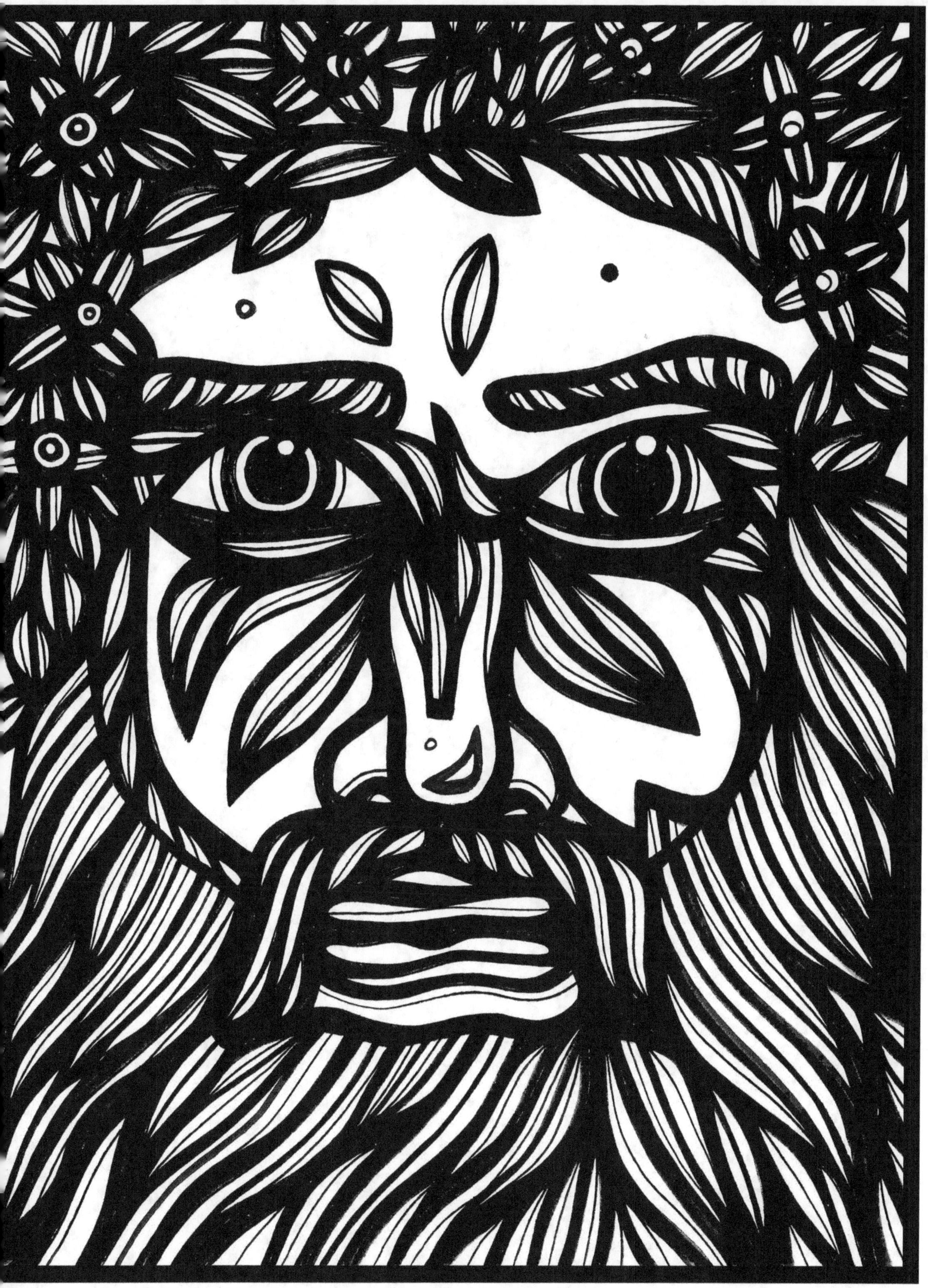

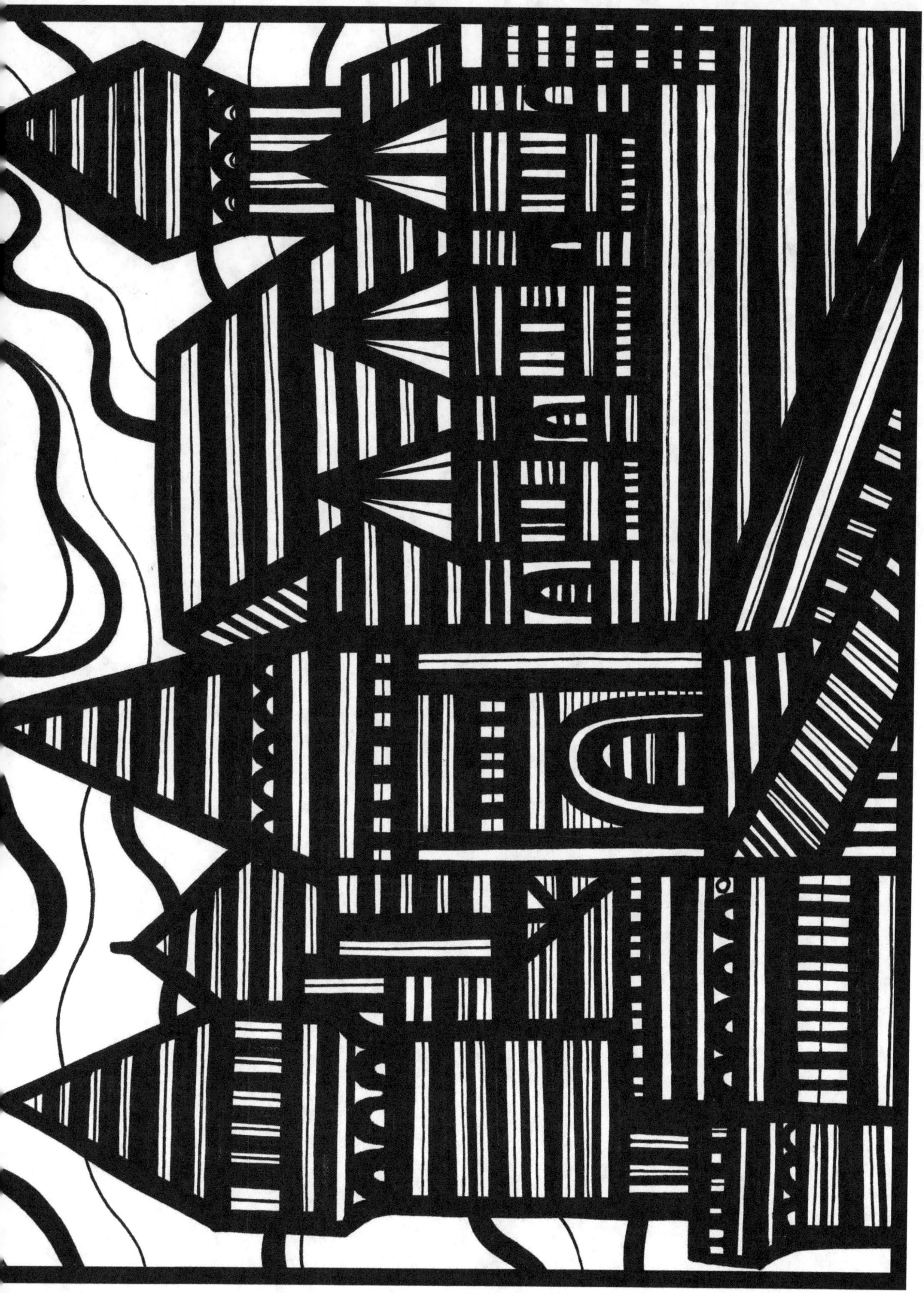

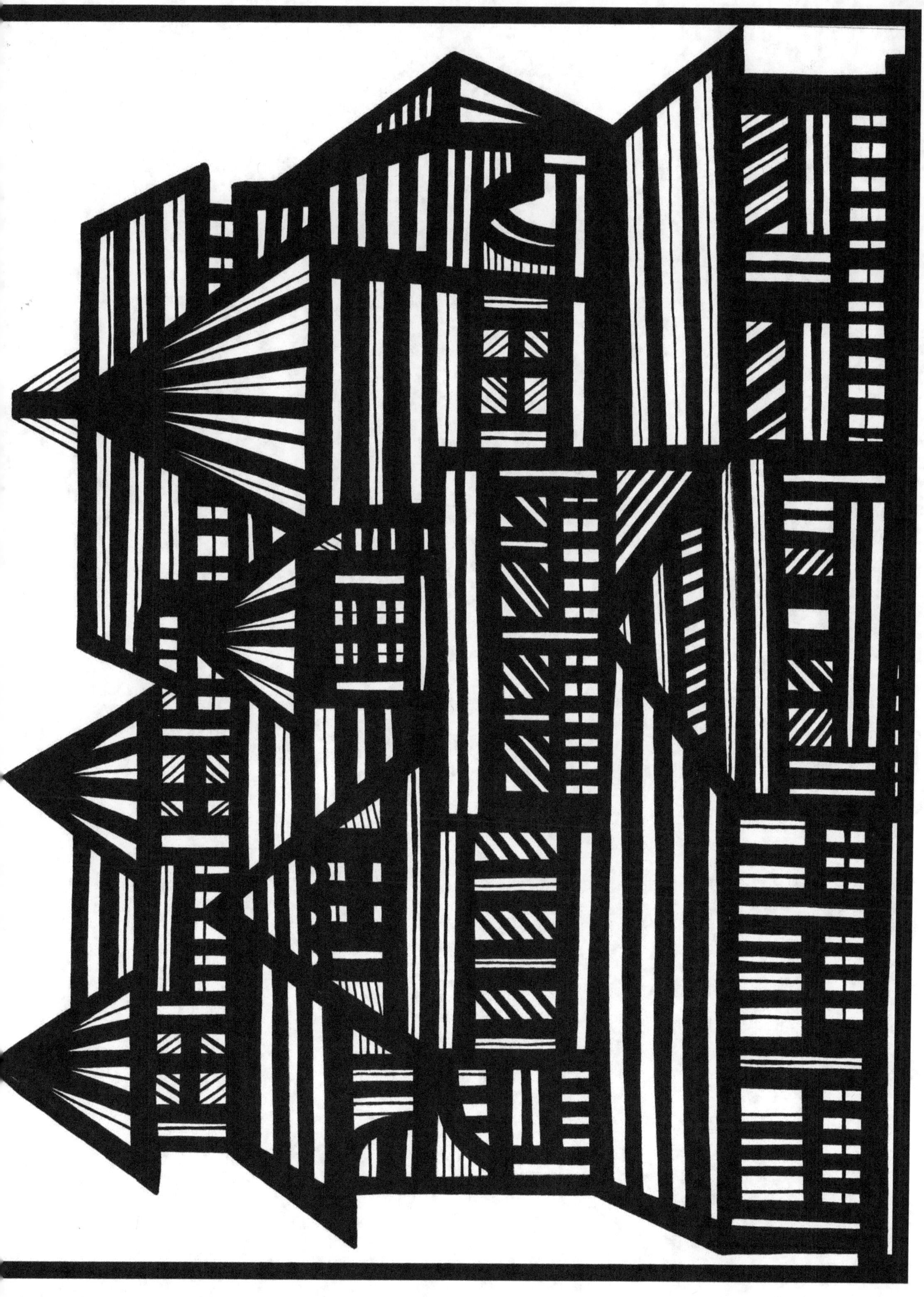

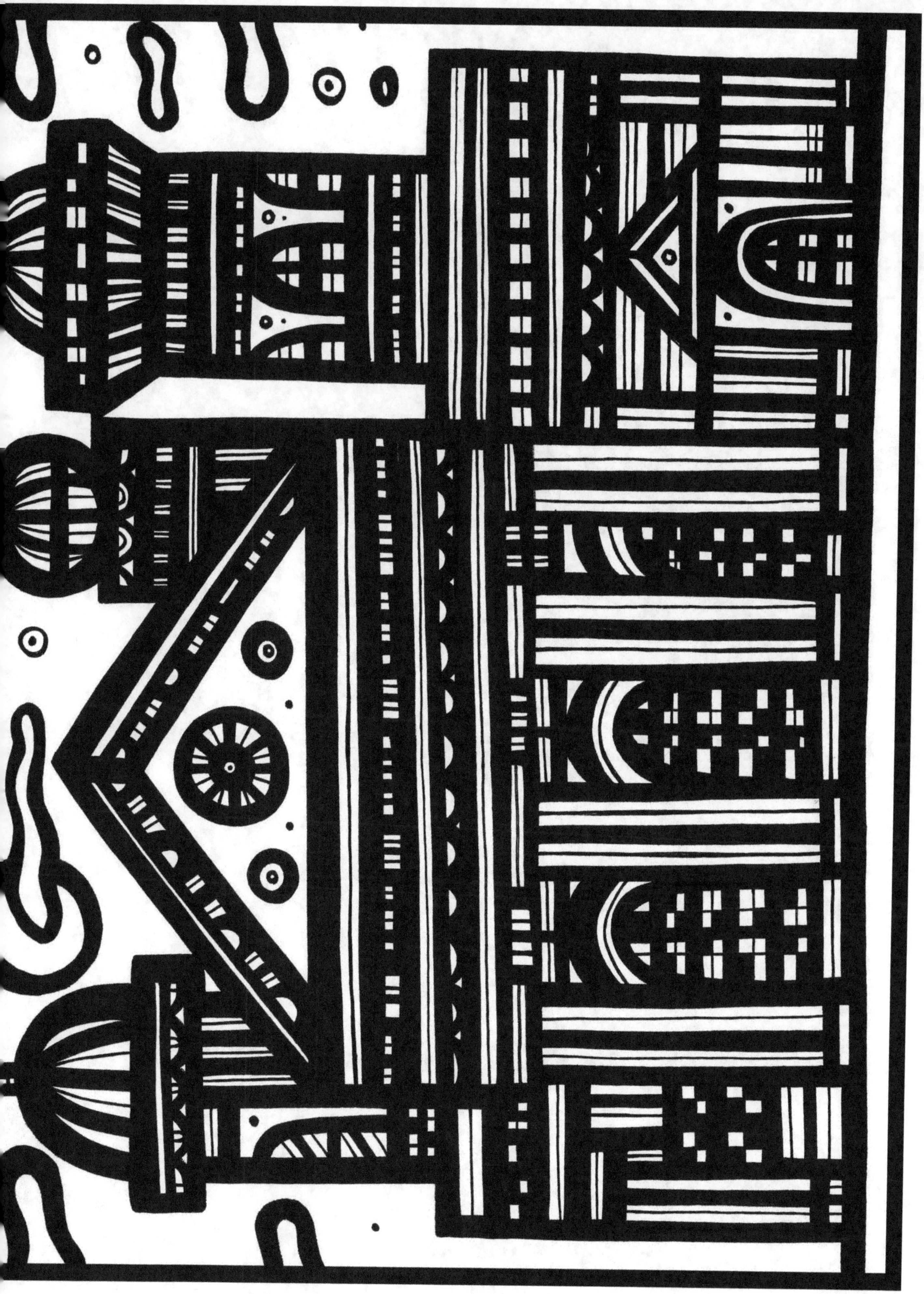

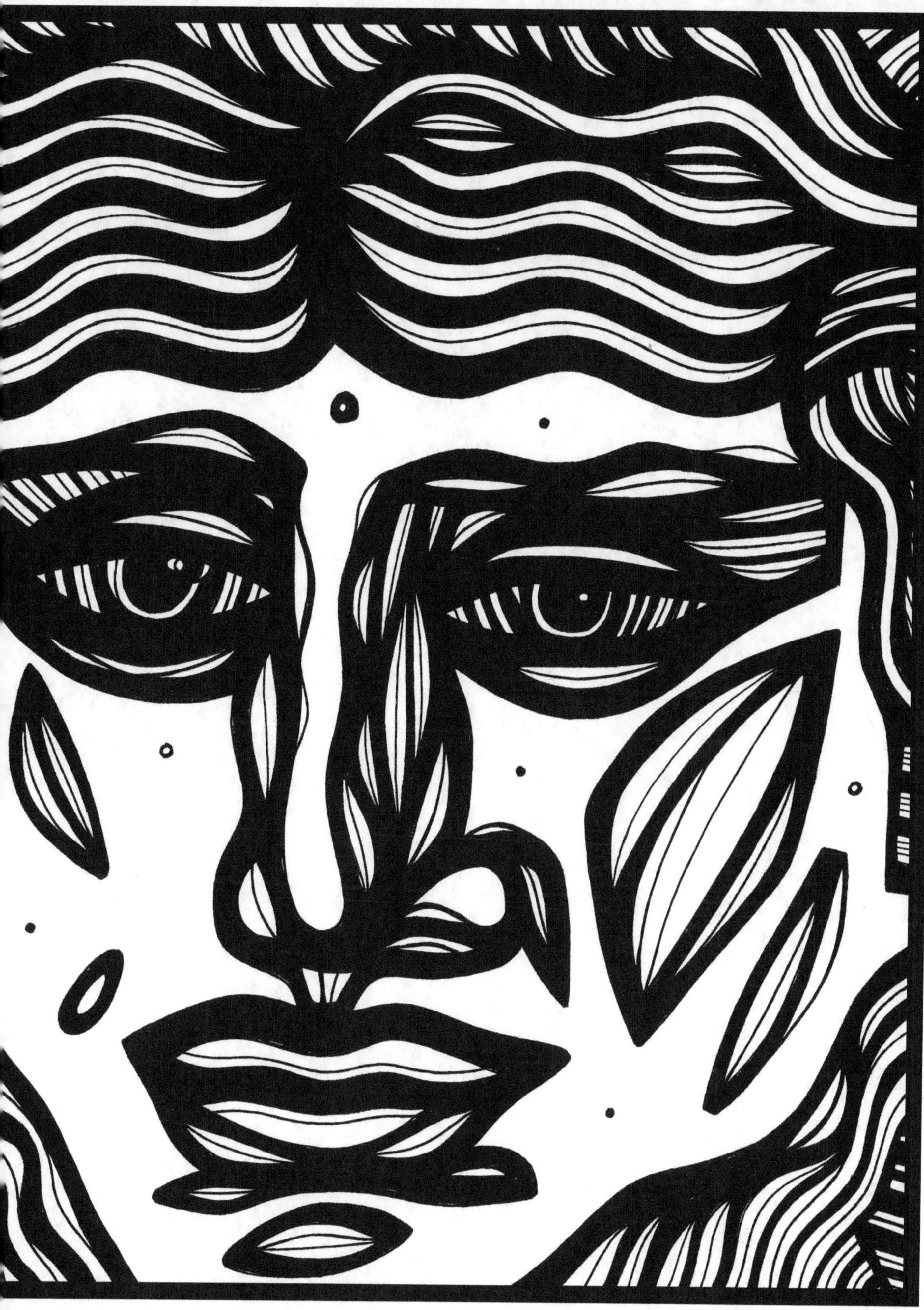

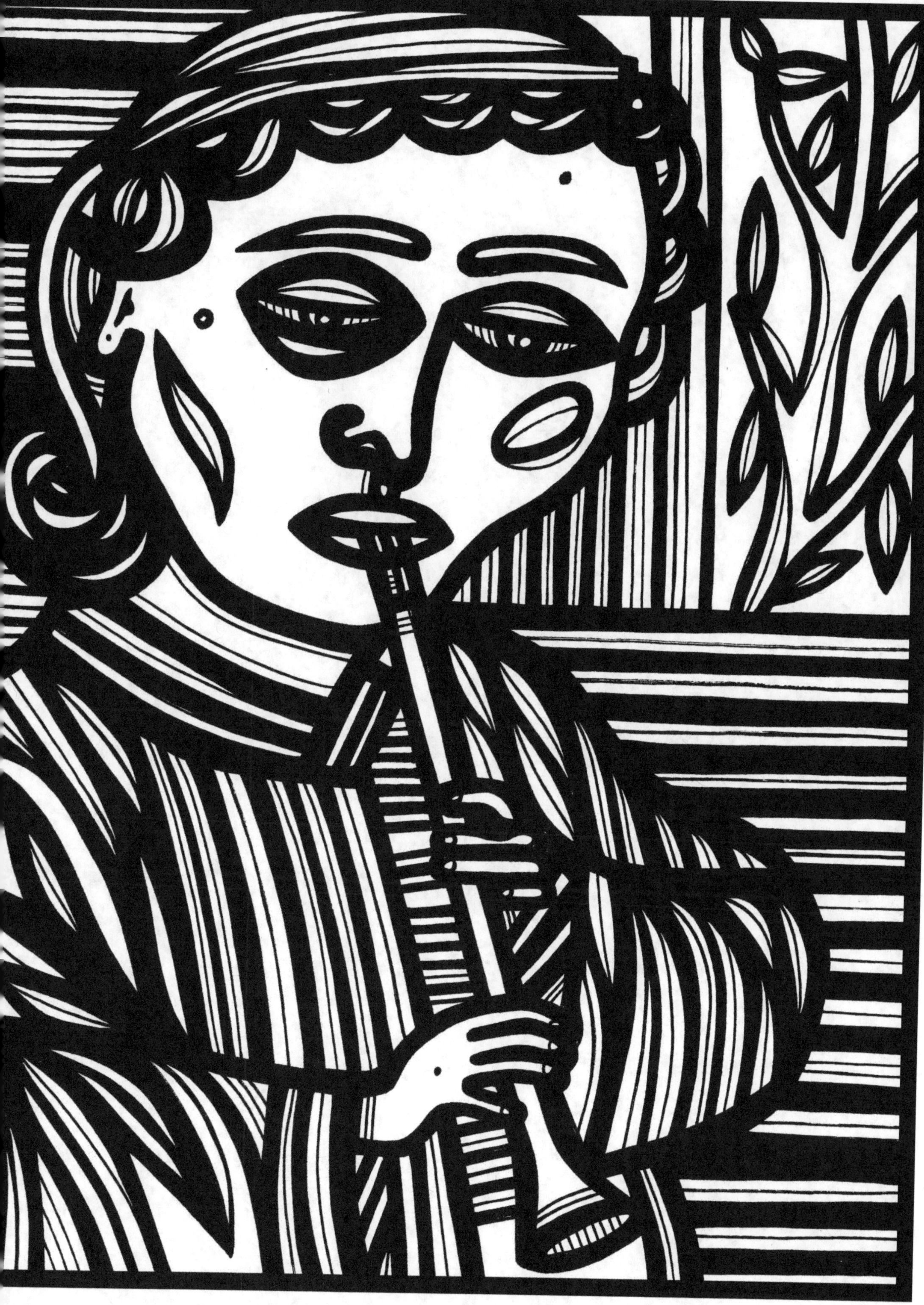

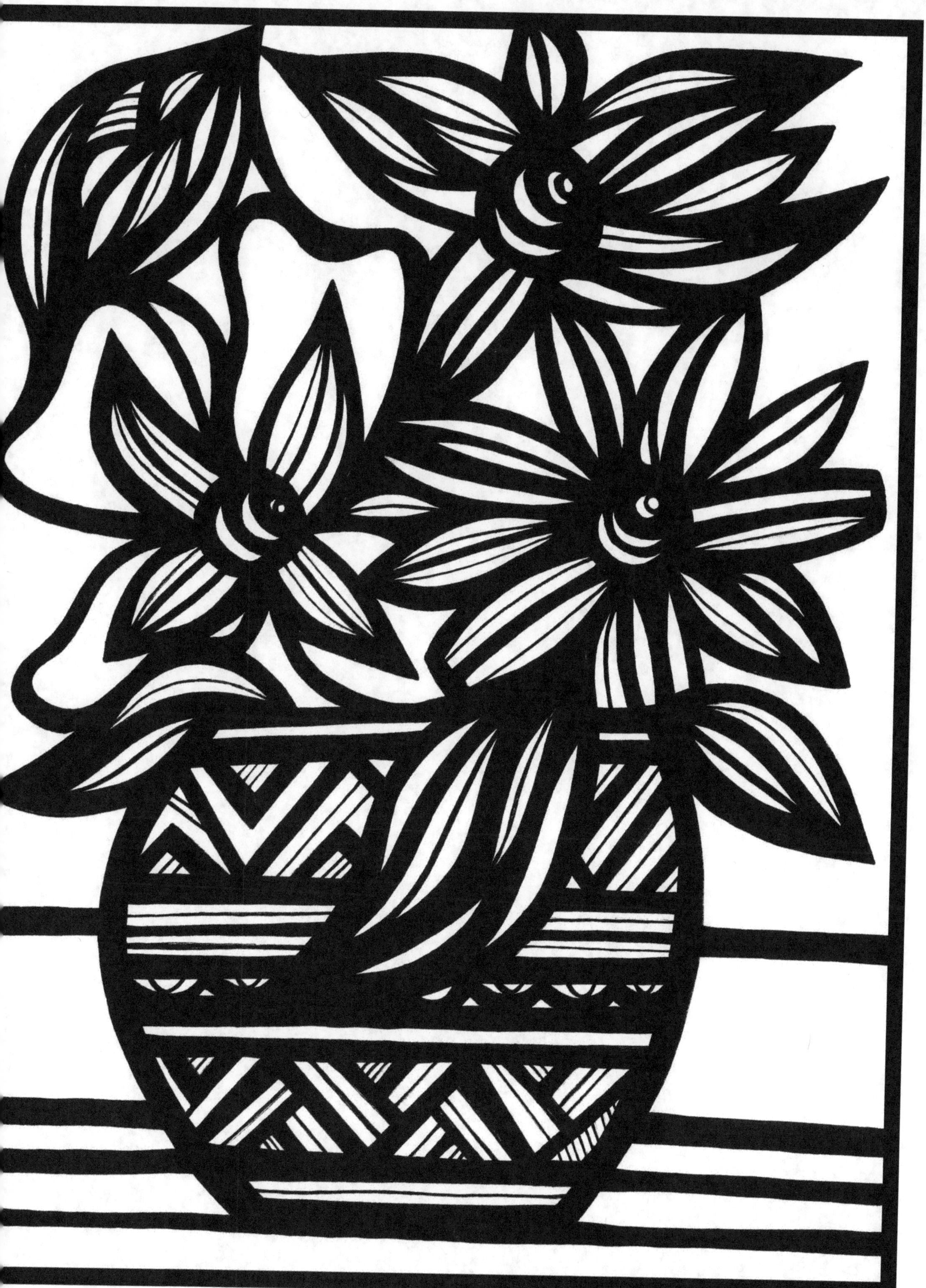

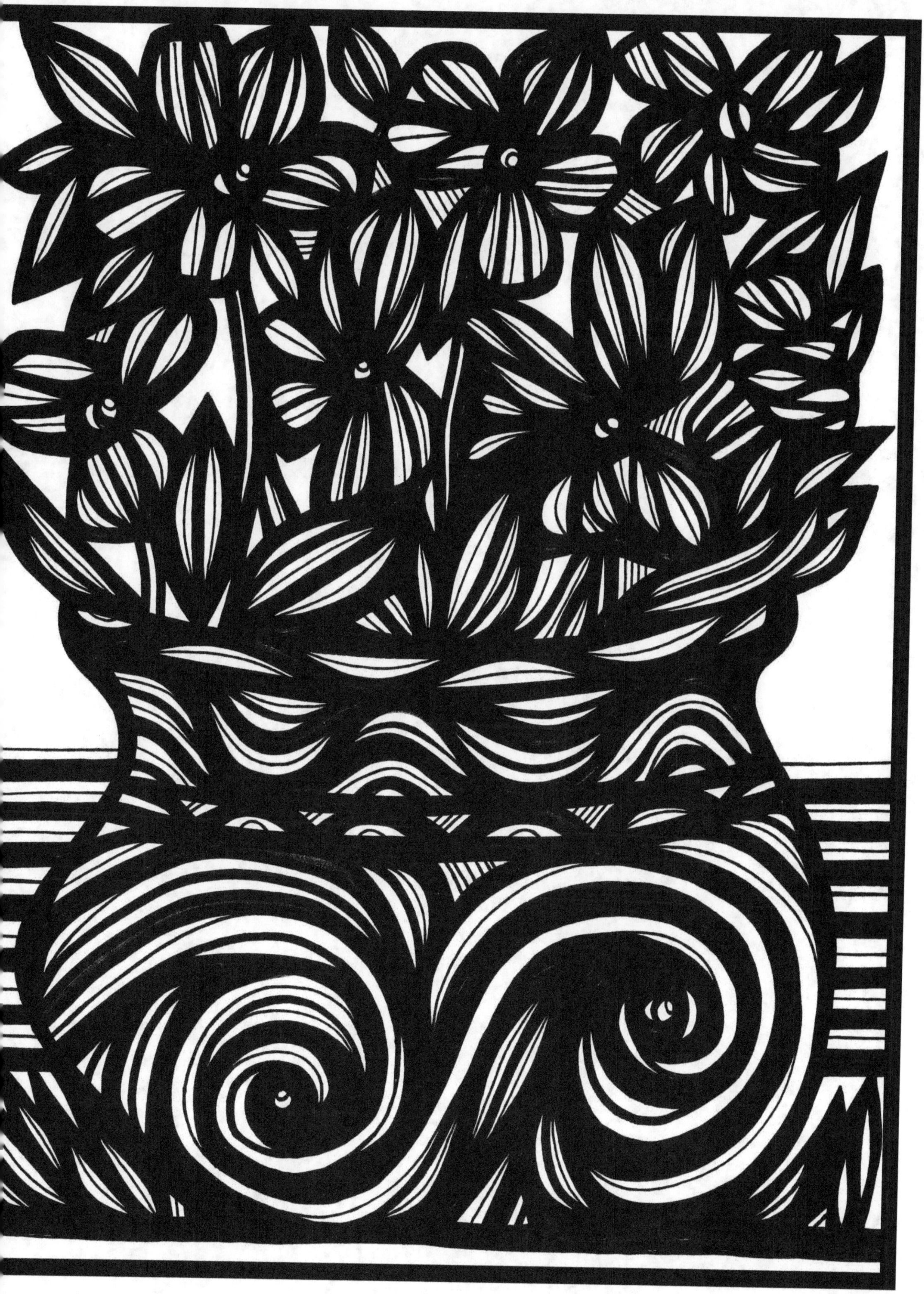

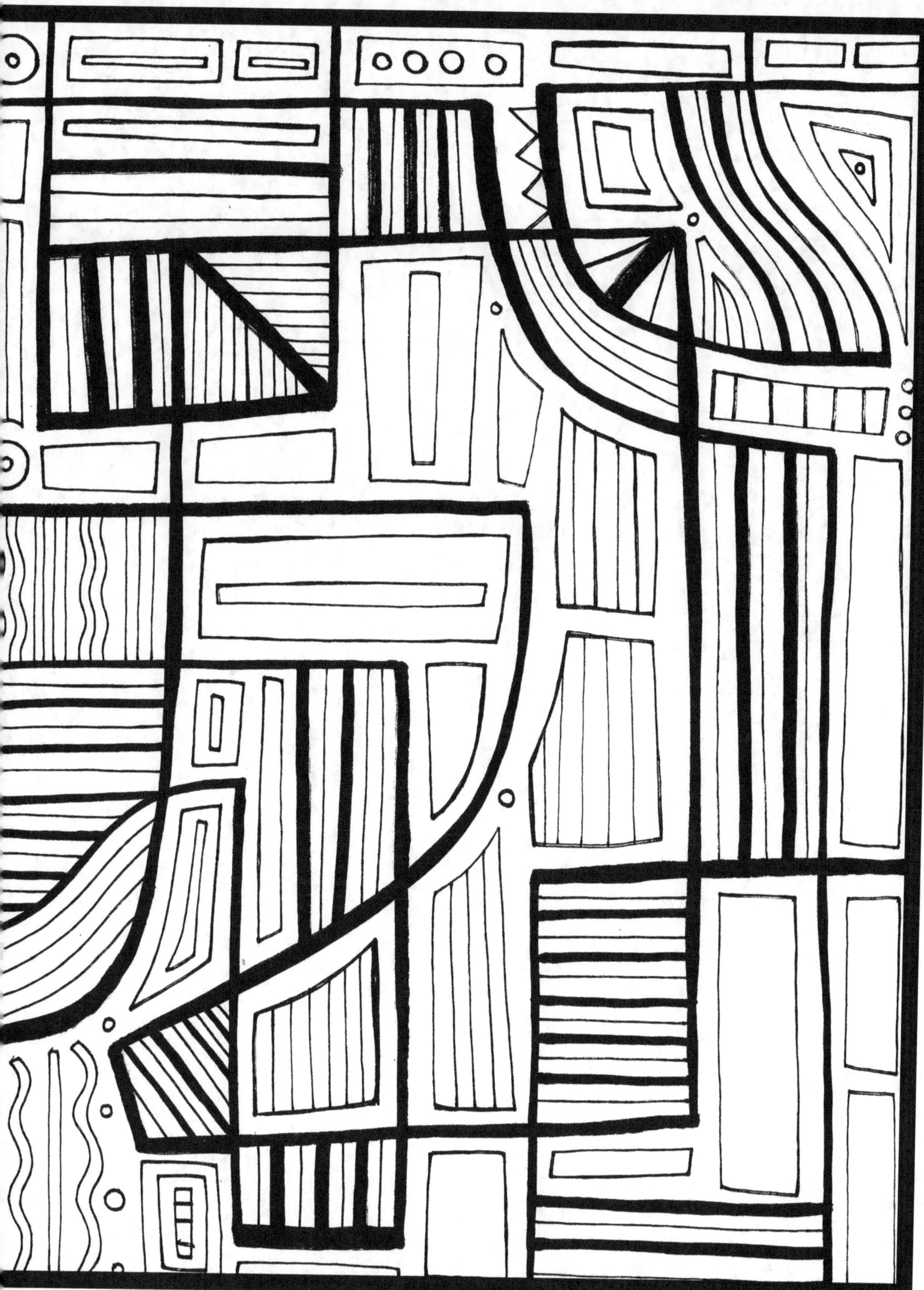

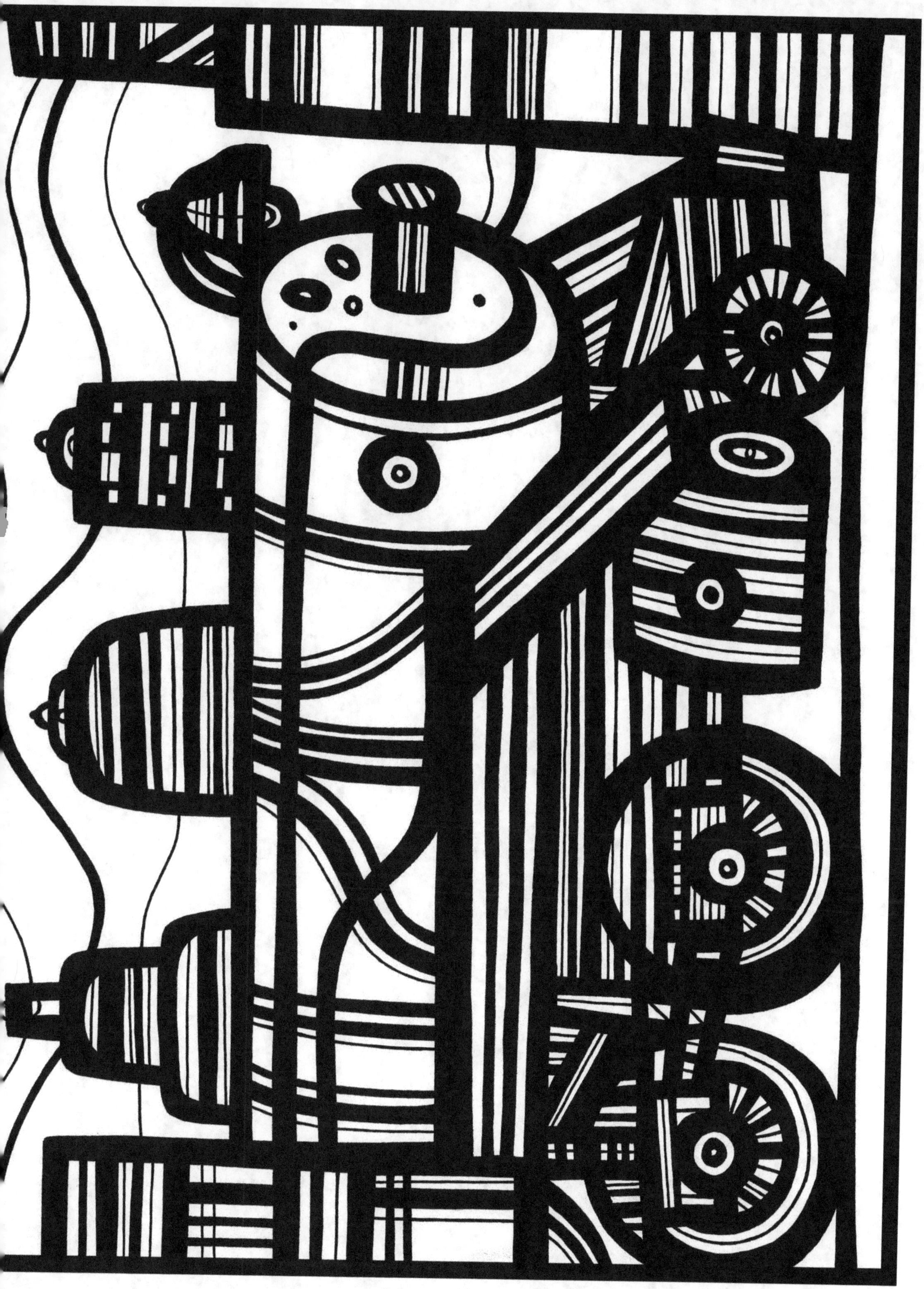

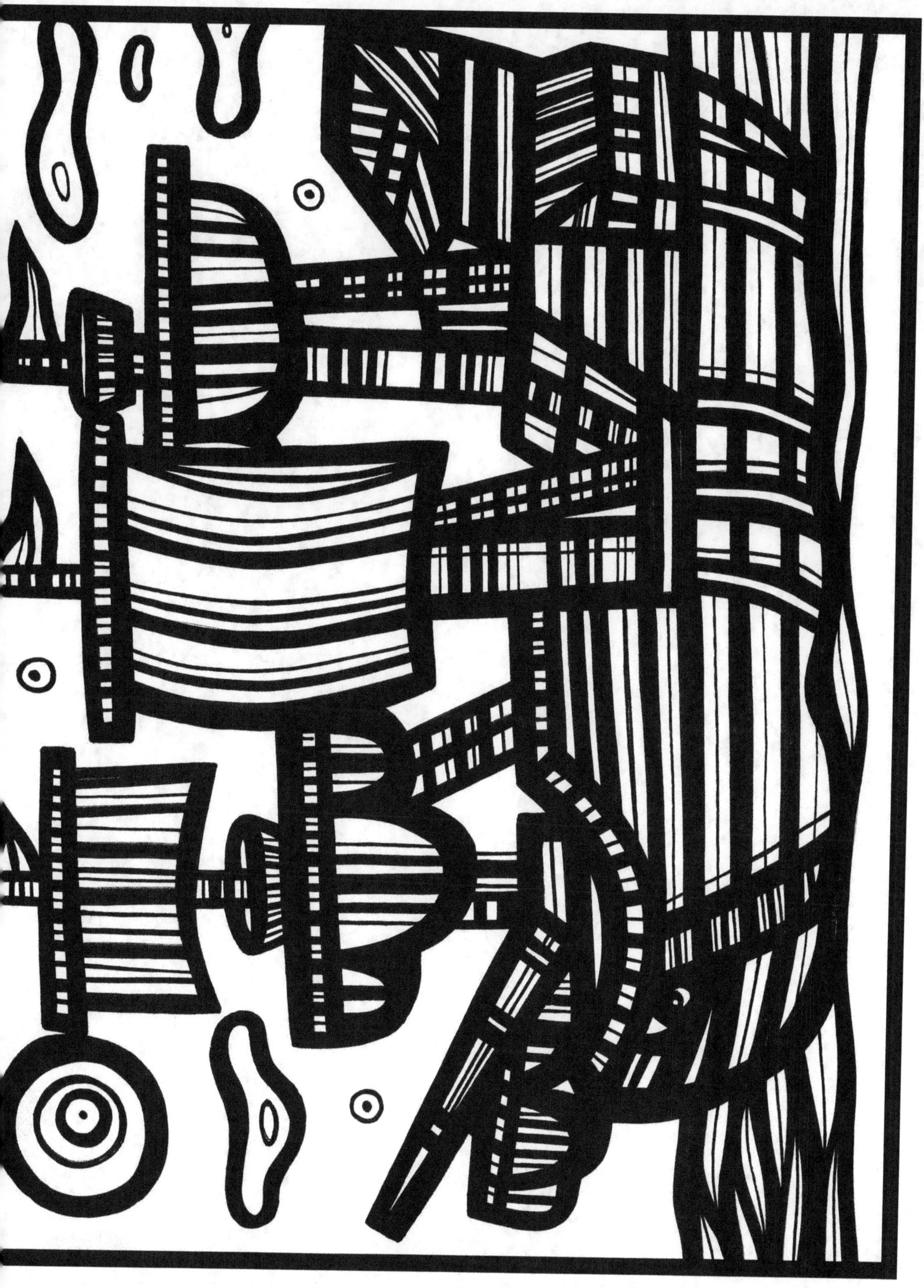

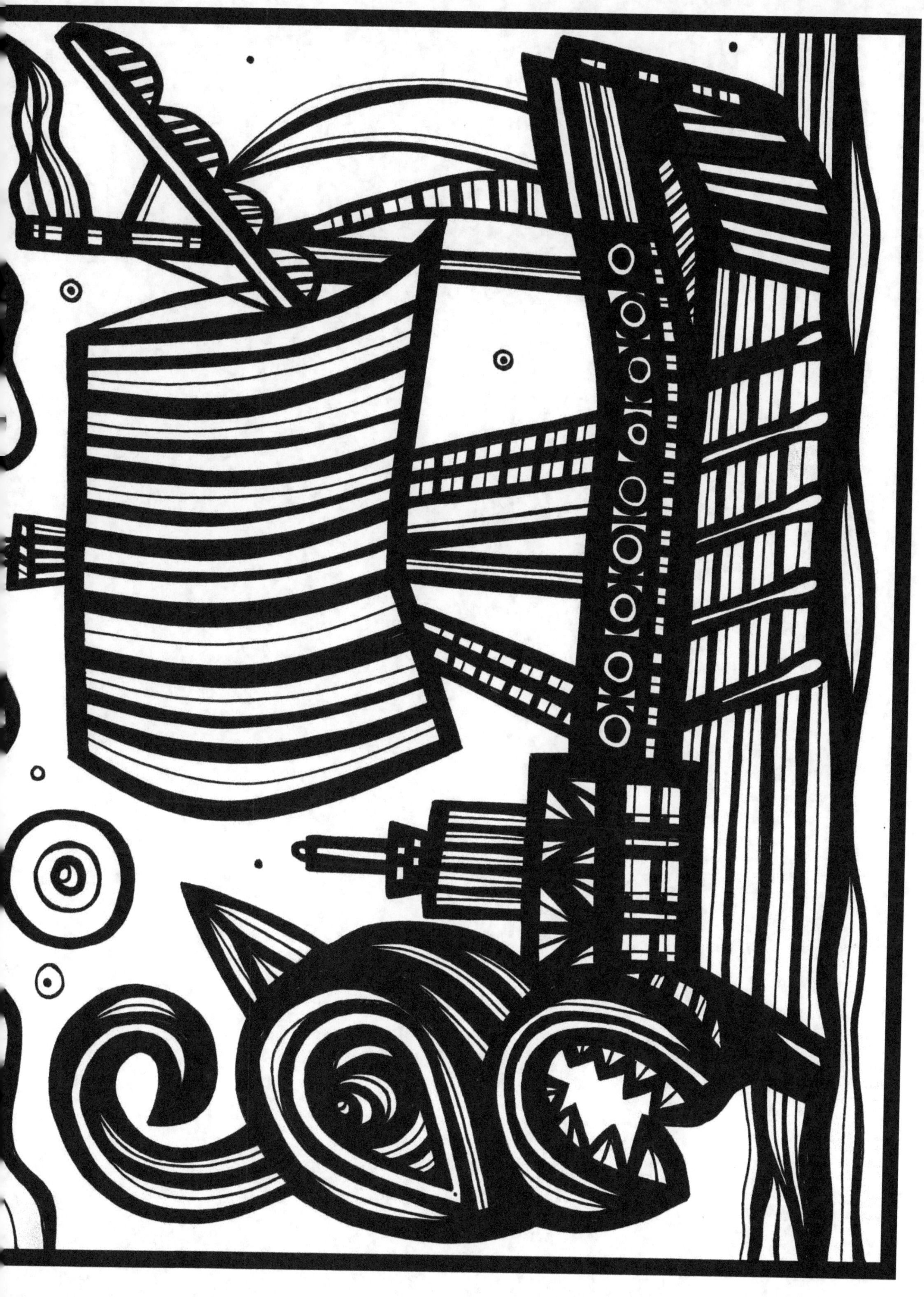

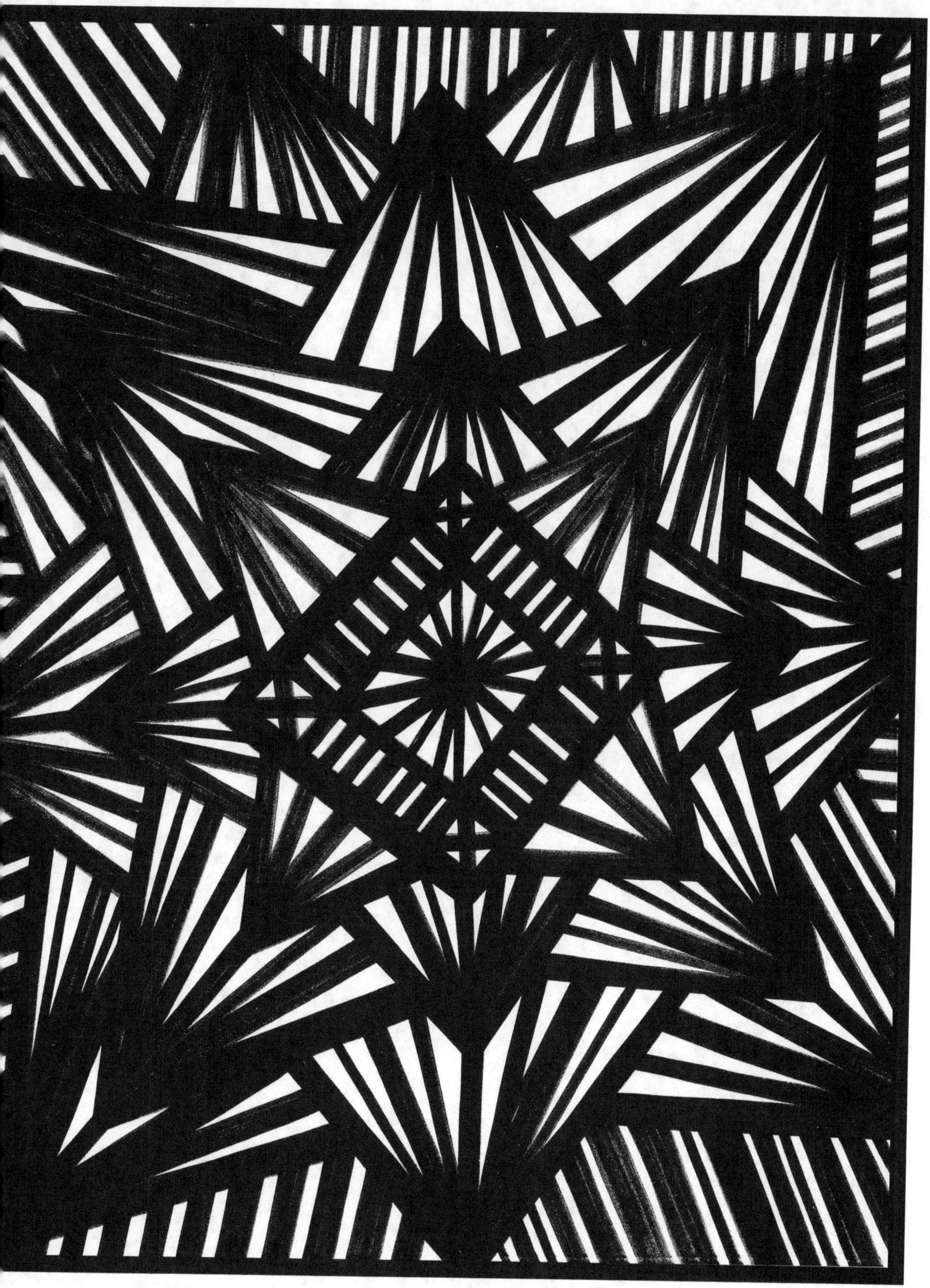

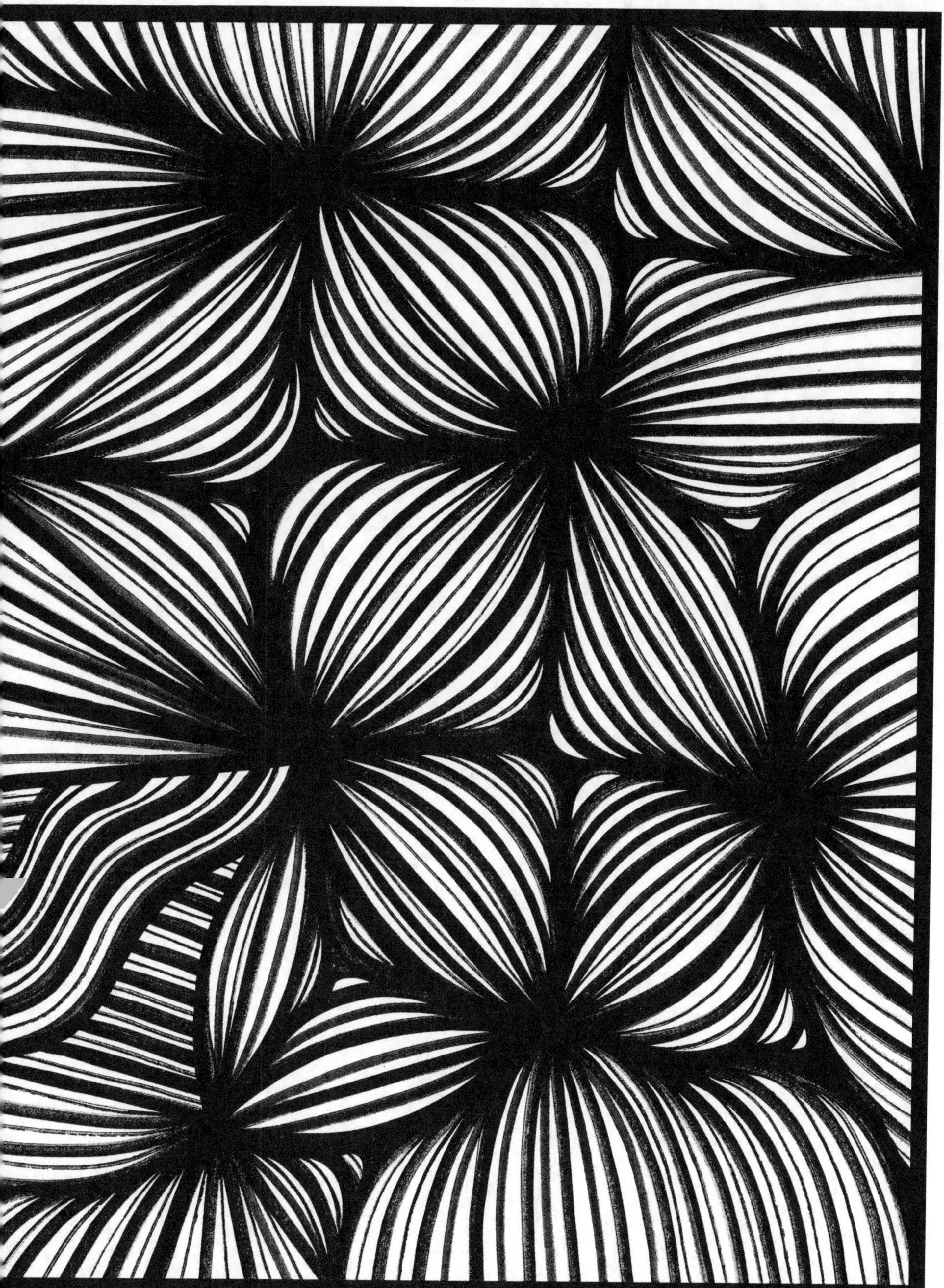

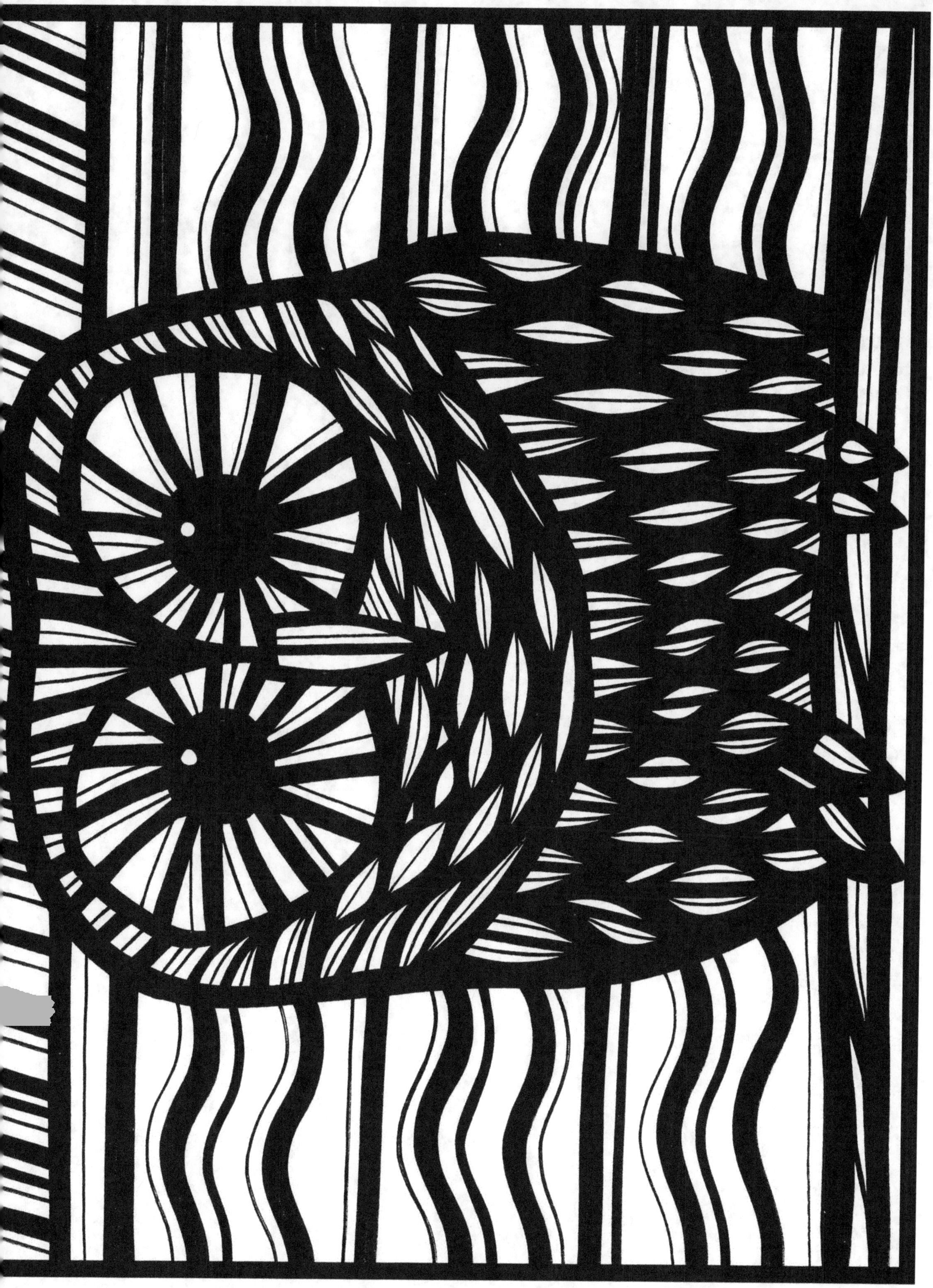

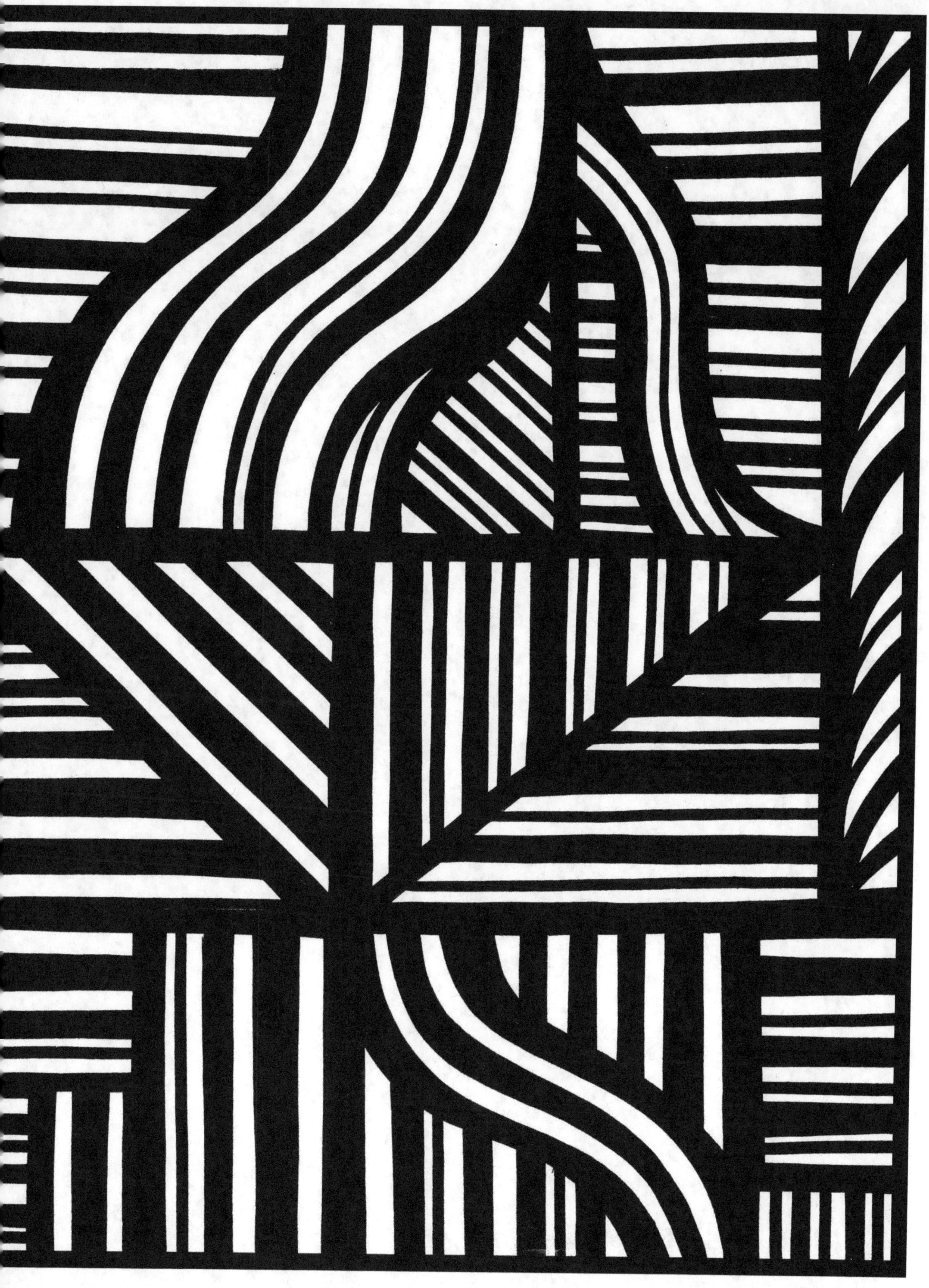

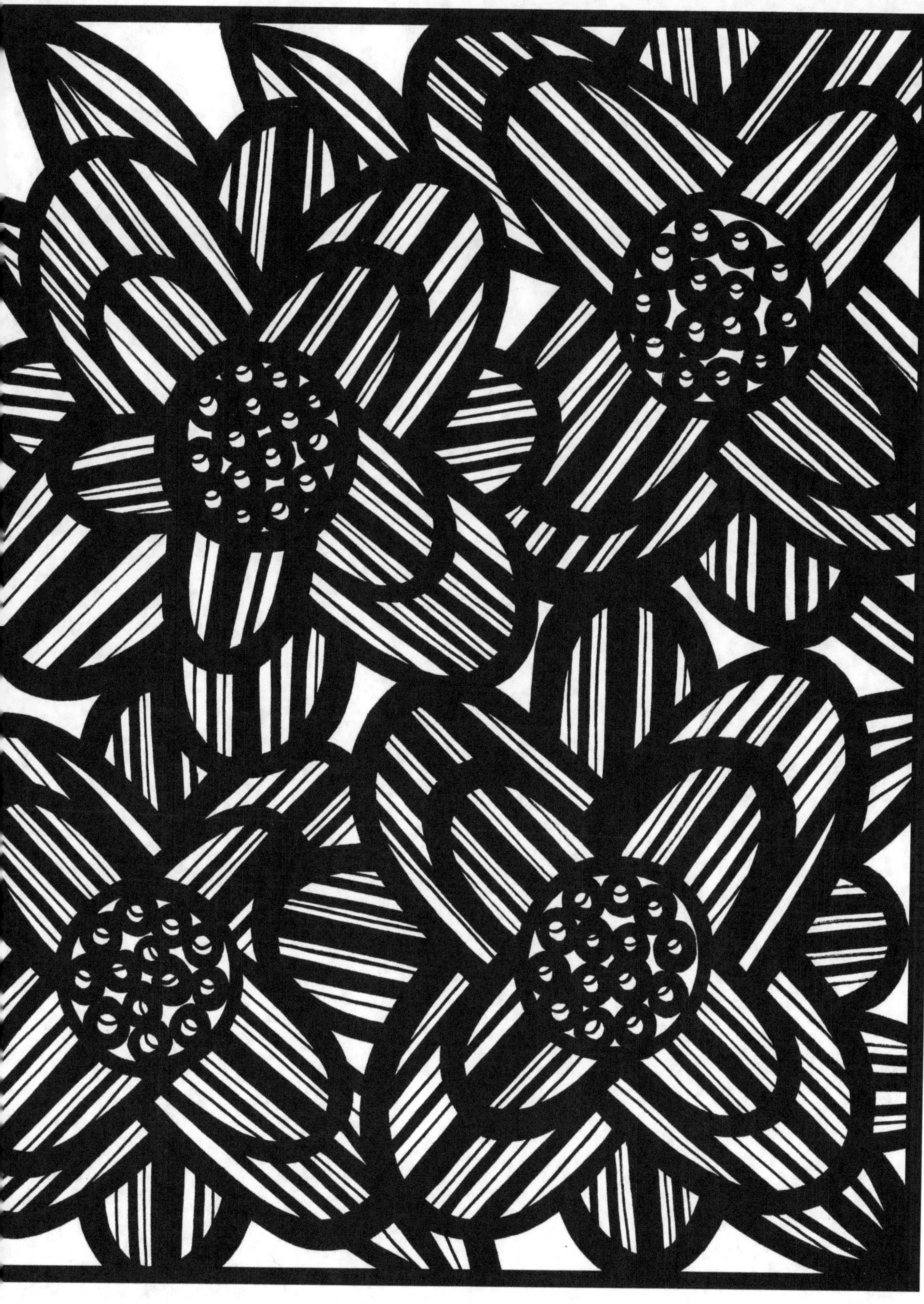

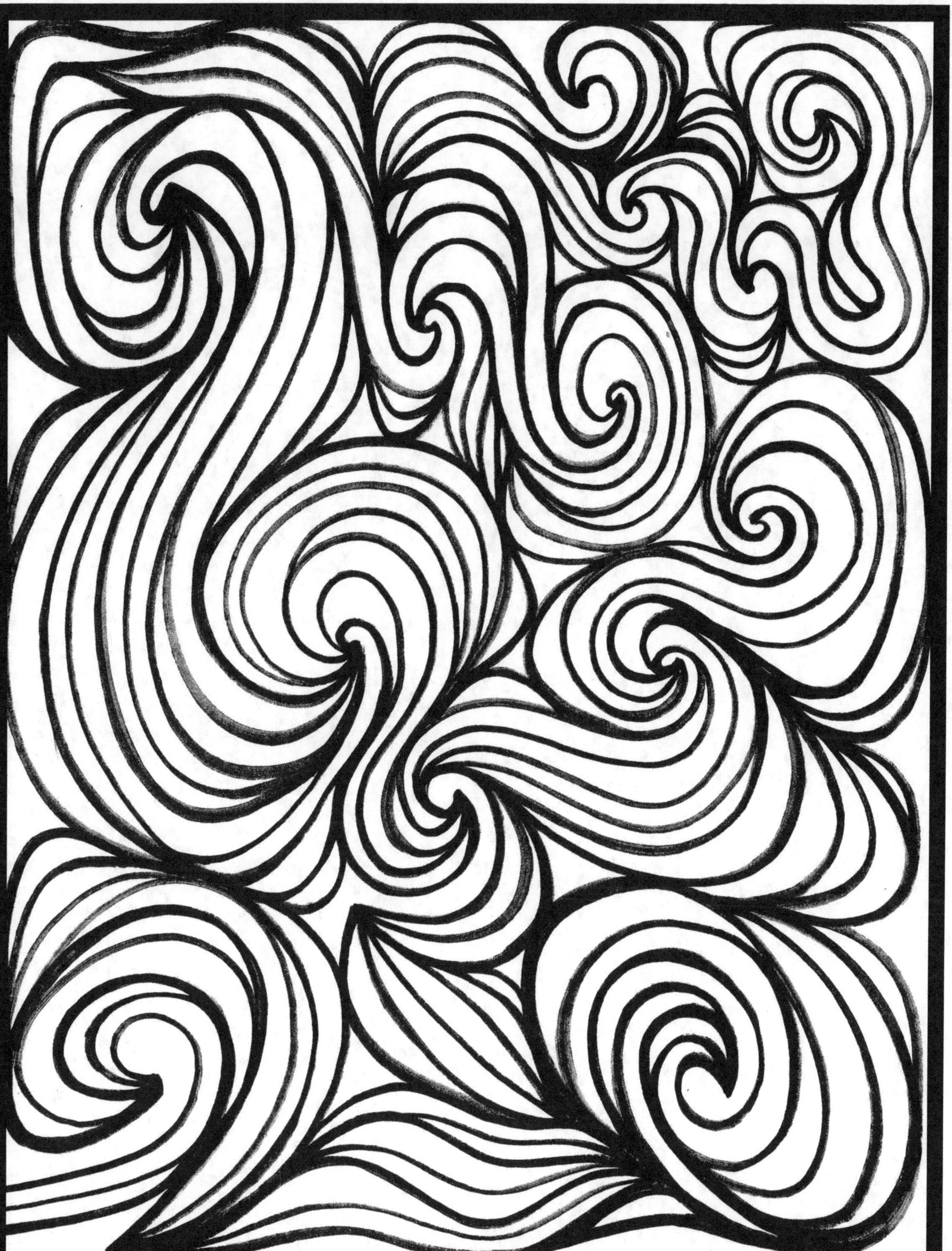

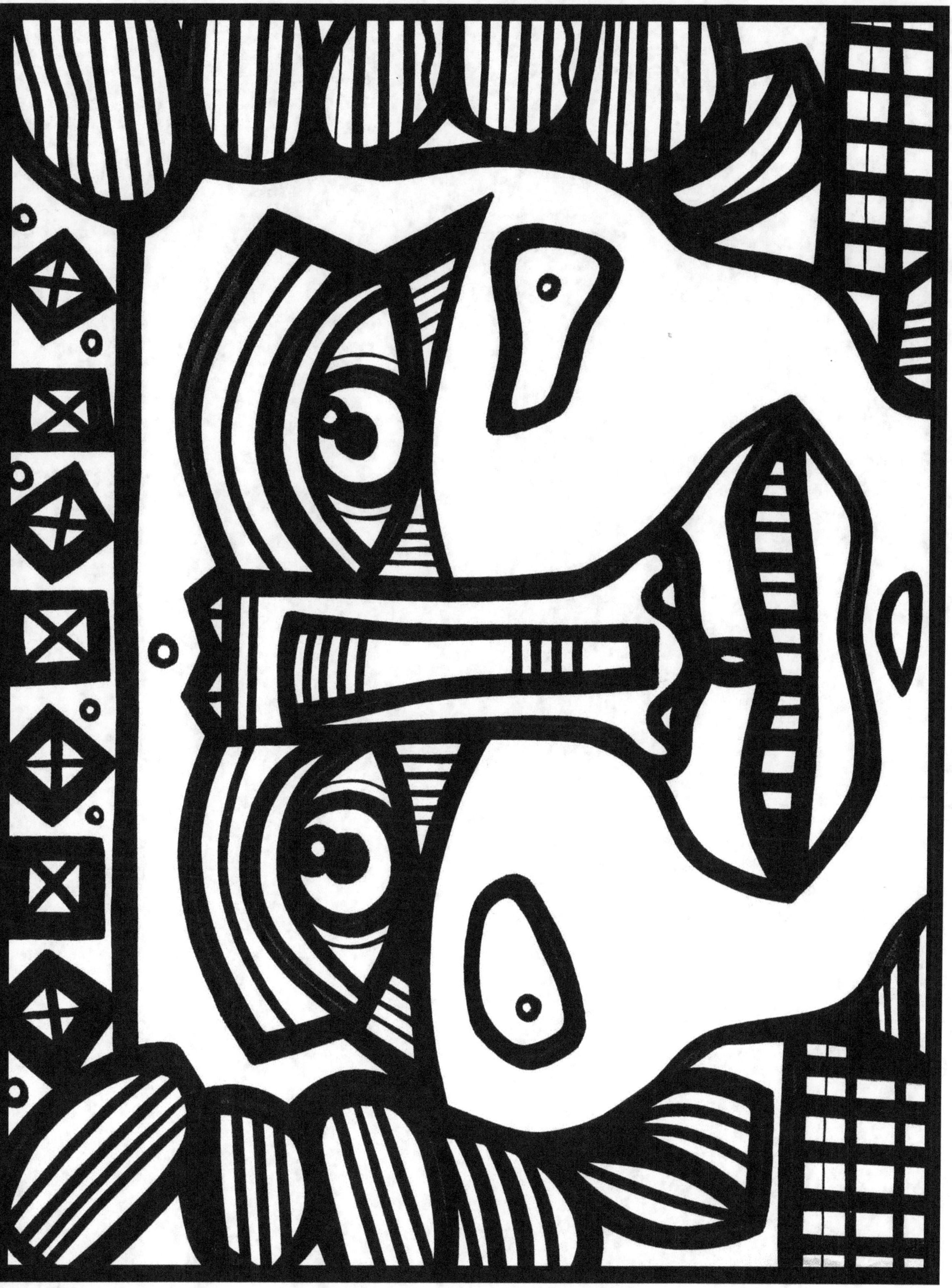

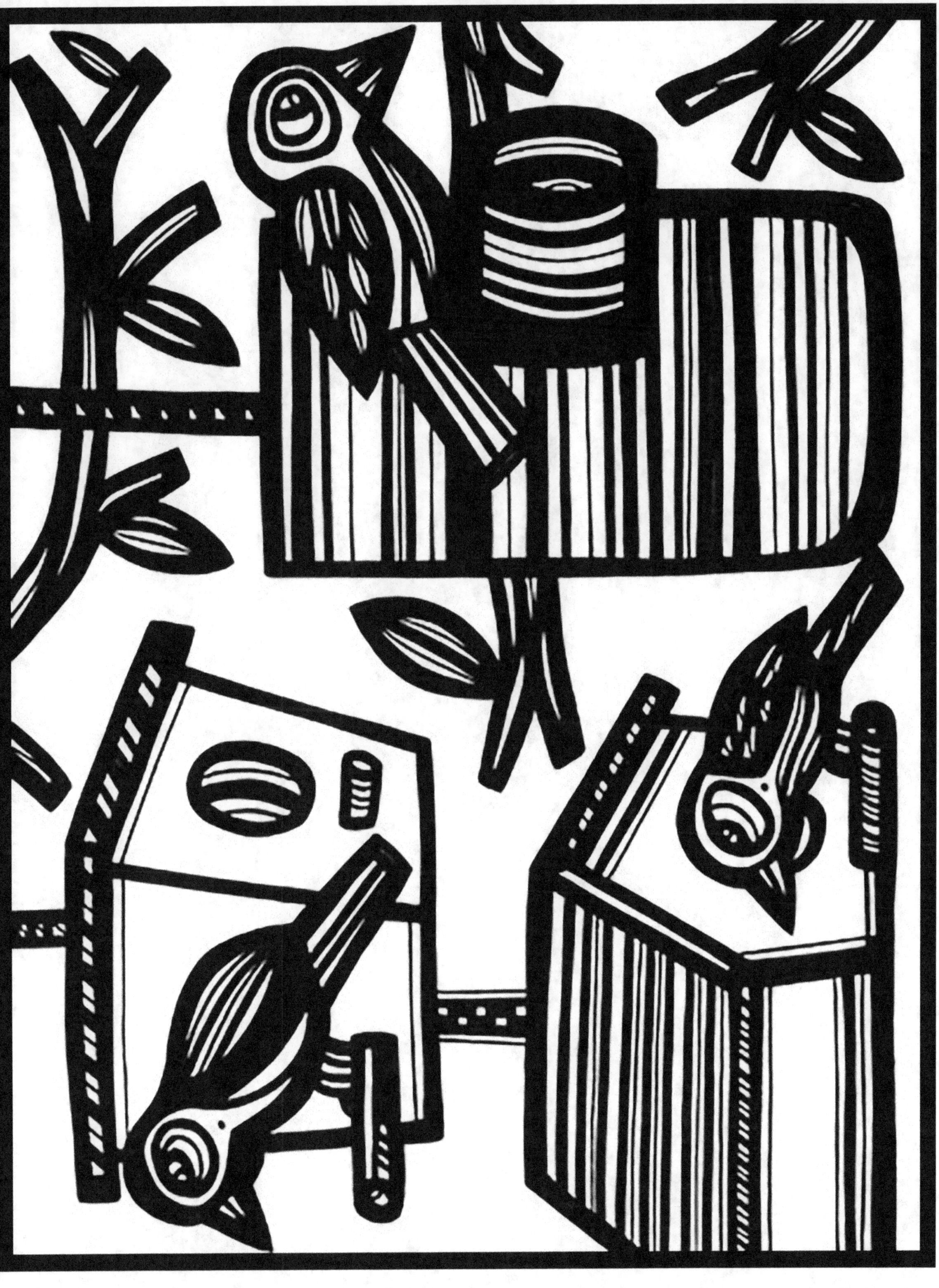

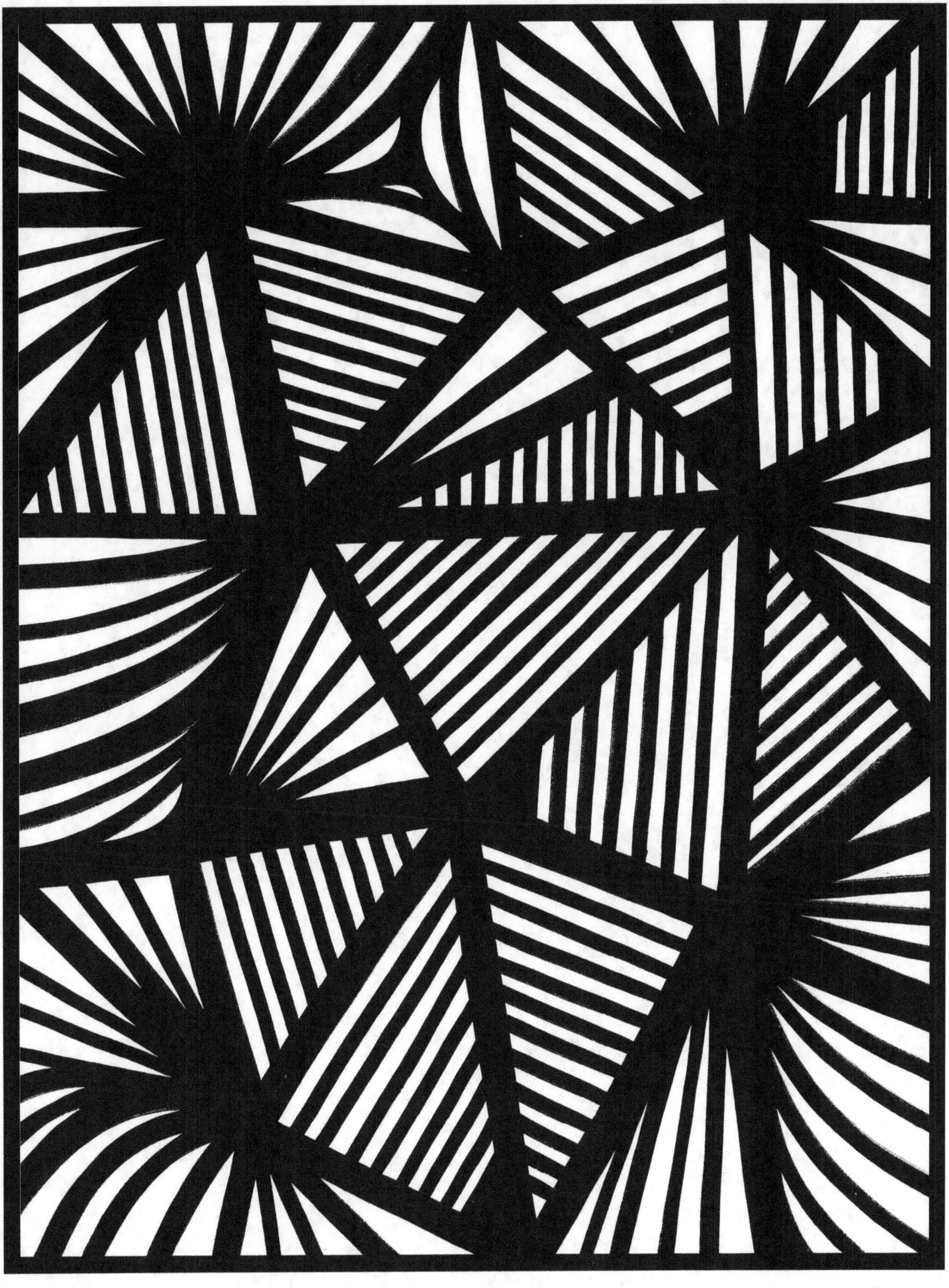

THE END,
THANK YOU.

COPYRIGHT 2020
BY EDDIE ALFARO
ALL RIGHTS RESERVED.

MORE BOOKS:
631ART.COM